DESIRE CAUGHT BY THE TAIL

By the Same Author

The Four Little Girls (Play)

DESIRE CAUGHT BY THE TAIL
a play by Pablo Picasso

translated by Sir Roland Penrose

Calder Publications Ltd   Riverrun Press
London   New York

First published in France as *Le Desir attrappé par la quieu* by Librarie Gallimard 1945. First published in Great Britain by Calder and Boyars 1970. Republished by Calder Publications Ltd 2000

ALL RIGHT RESERVED
ISBN 07145 0191 3

A catalogue record for this book is available from the British Library. Library of Congress Cataloging in Publication Data is available.

Typeset by Action Publishing Technology Ltd
Printed and bound by Watkiss Studios Ltd, Biggleswade, Beds.

FOREWORD

Is it because life is too short and human powers too limited that poets are not often painters or painters poets, or is there some contradiction between qualities needed in artist and poet which presents visual sensibility and powers of verbal expression from existing in the same man? In general it seems that those who – like the painter – live most acutely by the aid of their eyes tend to be unable to express themselves in words while those who can write down their thoughts are often incapable of using the plastic arts as a medium, so that it might be supposed that a damming up of the means of expression in the one case will lead to an overflowing exuberance and clarity in the other. In any case disapproval is usually expressed by the critics when an artist dabbles in a sphere which is not considered to be his own, and, indeed, few have found the time and the energy to make more than an occasional sally into the territories of another art.

We can think of the drawings of Victor Hugo and Lewis Carrol, the sonnets of Michelangelo, but it was particularly Leonardo who transgressed in this way and his answer to 'foolish folk' who criticised him is of particular interest: 'I am fully aware that the fact of my not being a man of letters may cause certain arrogant persons to think that they may with reason censure me ... They will say that because of my lack of book learning, I cannot properly express what I desire to treat of. Do they not know that my subjects require for their exposition experience rather than the words of others? And since experience has been the mistress of whoever has written well, I take her as my mistress, and to her in all points make my appeal.'

This attitude rules out the dilettante approach of those who take up some art as a part-time hobby, professional men, statesmen, doctors, and others who adopt an art as a kind of occupational therapy. This is not enough. To the artist all branches of the arts carry with them the same poetic reality, and it is only because of an overwhelming desire for total expression that one art can be called upon to fulfil the deficiencies of another. In a preface to the poems of Picasso, first published in the *Cahiers d'Art* in 1935, André Breton pointed out that Picasso has always expressed himself poetically, and the deliberate choice of using words rather than another medium has the same heroic quality that is found in the great strength and originality of vision of his plastic works. In fifty years of the most powerful creative production that we know of in our time, Picasso has been the leader of a revolution in the arts. 'An enterprise such as this requires all the resources of a passion which is self-sufficient, which disposes of a thousand tongues of fire.'

There is no barrier between the arts for Picasso. With prodigious talent, he has explored the possibilities of sculpture, photography, ceramics, lithography, and has in each case brought his own inventions and understood how to use the unfamiliar art so as to express more vigorously the drama of his perception of everyday life. Musicians are among his closest friends, and his love of music is expressed in the frequent appearance of musical instruments particularly guitars and flutes, in his paintings. The period when his association with musicians was closest was that brilliant epoch of the Russian Ballet, when, under the direction of Serge Diaghileff, ballets such as *Parade* and *Pulcinella* with Picasso's scenery and costumes, reached a rare perfection and showed the profound emotional effect that can be attained by a close collaboration between the arts.

Picasso has always been on intimate terms with a large circle of poets and authors. His friend and biographer, Sabartés, describes how in a conversation at Royan in the early days of the Second World War he said: 'When reading, you often notice that the author would have wished to paint and not write. One divines from the pleasure he takes in describing, as though painting what he says, a landscape or a character, that he really would prefer to be using a paint brush and colours ... Maillol, for instance, did not realise to begin with his vocation as a sculptor, as happens to many others. Some painters find their path from sculpture and many politicians would have sacrificed half their celebrity and their lives to devote the other half to literature.' Sabartés goes on to say that next day when he paid Picasso a visit he found that the usual daily output of new drawings and paintings had been stopped for a bout of writing.

Just as when a sculptor turns to painting we can trace in his works the sculptor's preoccupation with form, so the painter's poem will contain unusually vivid plastic imagery. 'He is a dream repainted in water-colours on a pearl. His hair is the art of the complicated arabesques of the rooms of the Palace of the Alhambra. 'Picasso's poetry contains a torrent of metaphor and the most unorthodox juxtaposition of words piled together creates in the mind visions of wide and varied appeal. There is an appeal to all the senses. In the following passage, for instance, it is sound that dominates the atmosphere. 'The noise of unfastened shutters, hitting their drunken bells on the crumpled sheets of the stones, tears from the night despairing cries of pleasure.' French shutters banging their hearts out against stone walls during the darkness of a winter storm, crumpled sheets, tears and cries of pleasure ... the picture grows, it is a living picture, the stones beaten by the shutters are associated with the crumpled sheets. It is as though these objects and passions infect each other and live in each other's attributes.

The same metamorphosis takes place frequently in modern painting. It can be seen clearly in Picasso's great mural *Guernica*, when the eyes of the women are shaped like tears, their pointed tongues are like knives piercing the air, the flames from the houses are like the crests of cocks, the dying horse has the surface of a bare field of

stubble while its mouth is like a fortress firing its last
defiant salvo. This world of association is inherent in the
forms which echo meanings beyond those they are
obviously intended to represent. Throughout this play,
language is forced into the same service. The dreamlike
sense which flows from Big Foot's soliloquies comes from
the influence of one word upon its unlikely neighbours.
Language has been forced into a state of instability and
like a spring uncoils with violence, hitting out on all sides
as it is released. What style could be more suitable to
Picasso in expressing the rage, the anxiety and the
nostalgia of Paris occupied by the Nazis during the depths
of the blackest winter of the war?

The play is a burlesque and often riotously funny, but
as Jean Cassou remarks: 'Death is always present in the
solitudes and caprices of the Spaniards.' The wildest scenes
of enjoyment end again and again in disaster. After the
opening discussion between the characters who are well
feasted and ready to explain the primary truths to their
cousin, the Curtains shake themselves with a night of
thunder in their incongruous belly and the stage is flooded
with will o' the wisps. In Act II their picnic ends with the
arrival of undertakers who bring in coffins, into which they
pack everybody, nail them down and carry them off. Act
III finishes with Big Foot's admirers covered with blood
and fainting on the floor. After universal and
unprecedented success in the lottery in which all the
characters, including the Curtains themselves, become
millionaires, Act IV ends with the fumes of chipped
potatoes filling the room until complete suffocation
follows. Finally the prize giving and dancing in the last act
is interrupted by a golden ball the size of a man, bursting
in at the window and blinding the entire cast.

The way in which annihilation recurs – and still the
play continues – has its parallel in the successive deaths of
the bull in a bull-fight when each time the spectators rise
to their feet in reverence and then settle down again to see

the same drama re-enacted. There is no unravelling of a plot. The sequence of the scenes and the coming and going of the characters suggest more the form of a ballet than a drama. The scenes in the corridor of Sordid's Hotel and the closing act are frankly like a ballet in conception. Another allusion to the bull-fight comes in Big Foot's reflection 'The guts which Pegasus drags behind him after the fight draw her portrait on the whiteness and hardness of the gleaming marble of her sorrow.' This is clearly the imagery of a painter, a sculptor and a Spaniard.

Picasso has usually written in Spanish. This play, designed for the amusement of his French friends whose lot he was sharing, was written in French but the language, as well as the images and background, have a strong savour of his native land. Here is another example which shows clearly the plastic qualities of the painter's vision: 'The titillations of crows, making the notched wheels of the machine for sewing and unsewing buttons, liven up the landscape so little that the grass grows on their flight and the shadows thrown by their wings do not stick to the wall of the church but slide along the cobble stones of the square where they break to pieces.'

Throughout the play there is an animism which not only makes living characters of the Curtains, the feet with their screaming chilblains, the Onion, the Tart, Silence and Anxiety, but also brings to life domestic objects and even their clothes. Thin Anxiety finds her white lace ball dress 'writhing in burning pain under the dust'.

But in spite of the richness of the imagery and the wideness of its poetic echoes there is no romantic tenderness. The pitch of irony, the wildness of the caprices springing as they do from the experiences of the appalling realities of the time, reach a point where our only possible reaction is a burst of bitter laughter. The experiences are not only of war, love and Sordid's Hotel but of everyday people and objects all living together as companions and characters in the same drama. It is a play of misery, discomfort, anguish, hunger and passion which is caught in the impossibility of its fulfilment.

The Tart gives us a clue when she says, 'You know, I met love. He has scraped knees and he begs from door to door. He doesn't have a sou and is looking for a job as a conductor on a suburban bus. It's sad, but go to help him. He'll turn on you and sting you.' But the situations that arise are full of a riotous humour and are a mockery of the daily trials of the time. The dominating theme naturally is food. Big Foot in praise of his girl-friend the Tart woos her saying, 'Your buttocks are a plate of cassoulet, and your arms a soup of sharks' fins, and your . . . your nest of swallows still the fire of swallows' nest soup,' and he declares that 'nothing is as good as a mutton stew . . . on a beautiful day when it is snowing hard.' When the Anxiety sisters sit down to their stew of Spanish melon, palm oil, broad beans, salt, vinegar and breadcrumbs – 'This great bouquet of terror and frights already begins to wave us good-bye.' It happens on the main sewer of their bedroom kitchen bathroom where Thin Anxiety finds that she is 'nothing but a congealed soul stuck to the windows of the fire' and that 'the sewing machine which turns the horses and lions of the tangled merry-go-round of my desires, chops up my sausage flesh and offers it alive to the ice-cold hands of stillborn stars, tapping on the panes of my window their wolfish hunger and their oceanic thirst. Fat Anxiety appears all dishevelled and black with dirt, rising from the bed linen full of potato chips, holding an old frying-pan, but the manner of address is on a very different plane.

Thin Anxiety	The Sun
Fat Anxiety	Love
Thin Anxiety	Aren't you beautiful

Our passionate hero Big Foot, as well as having a great appetite, is also no mean author, as we see when he produces a fine surprise for the Tart with her non-existent tea – his novel, and serves her with a slice of 'this great sausage' taken from page 380,000. He seeks throughout to adorn his lecherous passion, 'lighting the candles of sin with the match of her charms,' in extravagant metaphors and paradox and finally acclaims through music as the play draws to a close. 'Let us fold the dirty sheets in the face-powder of angels ... Throw flights of doves with all our strength against the bullets and lock securely the houses demolished by bombs' – a mock heroic Chaplinesque effort to put things right by doing the wrong thing.

The play is characteristically dated in the same way that Picasso dates his canvases and drawings even when he does not trouble to sign them, giving them the significance of a daily commentary on the events that have contributed to their creation.

It took him from Tuesday, 14th January, 1941, to Friday, 17th January, 1941, seated at his round table in his great draughty studio in occupied Paris during the dark and hungry winter of 1941, to sketch out this violent picture of the life around him. But it was not until 19th March, 1944, that Picasso's friends were able to give a first reading under the noses of the Nazis, who would have taken action against all concerned if they had discovered what was in progress. Here is the notice that appeared later in the revue *Messages*, Cahier II, 1944:

'The 19th March, 1944, at the house of Michel Leiris, a public reading was given of *Desire Caught by the Tail*, directed and produced by Albert Camus. The cast was as follows: Mmes. Zanie Aubier (the Tart), Simone de Beauvoir (her Cousin), Dora Maar (Thin Anxiety), Germaine Hugnet (Fat Anxiety), Louise Leiris (the Two Toutous), MM. Michel Leiris (Big Foot), Jean-Paul Sartre (Round End), Raymond Queneau (the Onion), Jacques Bost (Silence), Jean Aubier (the Curtains). George Hugnet in charge of the musical accompaniment.'

The readers, seated in an arc like a Cuardo Flamenco,

with Camus standing in a corner reading the stage directions, rose in turn to speak their words while the music came from a gramophone in a neighbouring room. About 120 people attended and among the audience were many distinguished artists, musicians, writers and actors, including Jean-Louis Barrault, Armand Salacrou, Paul Eluard and Picasso himself. The success of this first reading was so great that it was repeated five or six times and according to Michel Leiris it gave those present a feeling of an affirmation of liberty.

The same type of reading from a translation, was given in London three years later at the London Gallery in Brook Street and again proved extremely successful, for, although it might be possible to stage the play in a more conventional way, the author has made it possible for the best effect to be conveyed by a reading without scenery or costumes. This formula, admirable in its economy, calls upon the imagination of the audience in the same way as did Elizabethan drama with its sign boards instead of scenery.

A second reading was given in London in February 1950 at the Rudolf Steiner Hall, organised by the Institute of Contemporary Arts. The leading parts were taken by Valentine Dyall as Big Foot and Dylan Thomas as the Onion. This was followed by a reading of *An Island in the Moon* by William Blake, in which Dylan Thomas took the leading role.

A piece of writing as violent and original as this has few parallels, but it would seem that our English poet and painter, William Blake, though much younger and with a much less developed poetic style, was in a similar mood when in about 1787 he wrote *An Island in the Moon*. In fact there is an interesting resemblance in the form and the humour of the two compositions. But the more experienced and more evolved Picasso of 1941with his immense powers of expression and his determination to explore the unknown depths of consciousness brings him nearer to Rimbaud's conception: 'The poet makes himself *voyant* by a long, immense and reasoned unhinging of all the senses. All forms of love, suffering and madness; he seeks himself, he exhausts in himself all the poisons to keep only the quintessence.'

Of Picasso's prodigious creation, Paul Eluard has said: 'This man held in his hands the fragile key of the problem of reality. It was essential for him to see that which he sees, to liberate vision, to attain 'voyance'. He has succeeded.'

One of the most valuable aspects of this little play is that it helps us to see from a new angle the intimate processes of Picasso's creation. The verbal picture is as generous and original in its associations as the colour and form of his paintings. Realism is attained by looking 'behind the behind of the story which so deeply interests and grieves us,' and by the animation of objects combined with the process in which thoughts and abstract ideas take shape or become live personalities. 'The galloping pace of his love, the canvas born each morning in the fresh egg of his nakedness, crystallised into thought, jumps the barrier and falls panting on the bed. I have such wounds on my body; they are alive, they shout and sing and prevent me from catching the eight forty-five.' There is no abstraction in Picasso's mind, and this is true of all his work both plastic and literary, there is no idea of withdrawing into a quiet contemplation of static frozen beauty. On the contrary he humanises and gives life to the world within as well as the objects of the world without and in this audacious process of calling together a picture with wide sweeps of his wand Picasso the magician pauses to smile or wink at his audience.

Roland Penrose

DESIRE CAUGHT BY THE TAIL

CHARACTERS

BIG FOOT

THE ONION

THE TART

HER COUSIN

ROUND PIECE

THE TWO TOUTOUS

SILENCE

FAT ANXIETY

THIN ANXIETY

THE CURTAINS

ACT ONE

SCENE ONE

BIG FOOT.
> Onion, stop being funny; now we are well feasted and
> ready to tell the four primary truths to our cousin.
> Once and for all we must explain the causes of the
> consequences of our adulterous marriage; we must not
> hide its muddy soles and its wrinkles from the
> gentleman rider, however respectful he may be of
> propriety.

ROUND PIECE.
> Just a moment, just a moment.

BIG FOOT.
> No good, no good.

THE TART.
> Enough, that's enough, quiet down and let me talk.

BIG FOOT.
> Well.

ROUND PIECE.
> Well, well.

THE TWO TOUTOUS.
> Gua, gua.

BIG FOOT.
I wanted to say that if we want to come to an understanding at last concerning the price of furniture and the letting of the villa, we must, and absolutely with one accord, strip Silence immediately of his suit and put him naked in the soup which in parenthesis is beginning to cool off at a frantic pace.

FAT ANXIETY.
I ask for permission to speak.

THIN ANXIETY.
Me too, me too.

SILENCE.
Will you shut up.

THE ONION.
The choice of this hotel for private meetings in a walled-in public place such as this has not yet been decided, and we ought to examine this very unsettled question in the microscope, bit by bit and between the finest down of its hairs.

BIG FOOT.
Don't hide so cunningly behind the behind of the story which so deeply interests and grieves us; the choice of witnesses has been made, holy mackerel! and well made. And as for us, we'll be quite happy to cut our pattern from the shadow cast by the bills owing to the landlord.

SILENCE. (Taking off his clothes)
God, it's hot!

THE COUSIN.
I have already put some coal on, just recently, but it doesn't heat up. What a bloody bore.

THE ONION.
That chimney must be swept tomorrow; it smokes.

ROUND PIECE.
It would be better to build a fine new young one next year ... and that done, no more mice, no more black beetles.

THE TART.
Me, I like central heating better; it's cleaner.

THIN ANXIETY.
Oh! How bored I am ...

FAT ANXIETY.
Shut up, we're guests here.

ROUND PIECE.
To bye-byes, to bye-byes ... Do you know what time it is? A quarter after two.

SCENE TWO

(Change of lighting to storm)

THE CURTAINS. (Shaking themselves)
What a storm! What a night! Truly and certainly a
night for cuddling ... a Chinese night, pestilential
night in Chinese porcelain ... a night of thunder in
my incongruous belly. (Laughing and farting.)

(Music by Saint Saens: 'La Danse Macabre'. Underfoot
the rain begins to pour upon the floor and will-o-the-
wisps run about the stage.)

*

ACT TWO

SCENE ONE

(A corridor in SORDID's Hotel.)

(The two feet of each guest are in front of the doors of their rooms, writhing in pain.)

THE TWO FEET OF ROOM NO. 3.
My chilblains, my chilblains, my chilblains.

THE TWO FEET OF ROOM NO. 5.
My chilblains, my chilblains.

THE TWO FEET OF ROOM NO. 1.
My chilblains, my chilblains, my chilblains.

THE TWO FEET OF ROOM NO. 4.
My chilblains, my chilblains, my chilblains.

THE TWO FEET OF ROOM NO. 2.
My chilblains, my chilblains, my chilblains.

(The transparent doors light up and the dancing shadows of five monkeys eating carrots appear. Complete darkness)

*

SCENE TWO

(Same scenery)

(TWO HOODED MEN bring an immense bathtub full of soap suds on to the stage, in front of the doors of the corridor. After a piece for violin from 'La Tosca', from the bottom of the bathtub rise the heads of BIG FOOT, THE ONION, THE TART, HER COUSIN, ROUND PIECE, THE TWO BOW-WOWS, SILENCE, FAT ANXIETY, THIN ANXIETY, THE CURTAINS.)

THE TART.
Well washed, well rinsed, clean, we are like mirrors of ourselves and ready tomorrow and every day once more to start the same merry-go-round.

BIG FOOT.
Tart, I see you!

THE ONION.
I see you.

ROUND PIECE.
I see you, I see you, hussy!

BIG FOOT. (Speaking to THE TART)
You have a pretty leg and a well turned navel, an elegant waist and perfect tits, maddening eyebrows, and a mouth which is a nest of flowers, your hips a sofa, and the spring seat of your belly a box at a bull-fight in the arena of Nimes, your buttocks a plate of cassoulet, and your arms a soup of sharks' fins, and your —— and your nest of swallows still the fire of swallow's nest soup. But my honey, my duck, my pet, you drive me crazy, crazy, crazy, crazy.

THE ONION.
Old strumpet! Little whore!

ROUND PIECE.
Where do you think you are, old man, at home or in a brothel?

HER COUSIN.
If you go on like this, I shall refuse to wash and I shall leave immediately.

THE TART.
Where is my soap? My soap? My soap?

BIG FOOT.
The hussy!

THE ONION.
Yes, the hussy!

THE TART.
How good this soap smells, oh, how good it smells!

ROUND PIECE.
Take your sweet smelling soap and stuff it up.

BIG FOOT.
Beautiful baby, may I rub you?

ROUND PIECE.
What a wench!

(THE TWO BOW-WOWS, yelping, lick everybody. They jump out of the bathtub, covered with soap suds, and the bathers, dressed like everybody of this period, come out of the tub. THE TART alone gets out stark naked except for her stockings. They bring in baskets of food, bottles of wine, tablecloths, napkins, knives, forks. They prepare a great 'al fresco' lunch. In come some undertakers with coffins, into which they dump everybody, nail them down and carry them off.)

*

ACT THREE

ACT THREE

SCENE ONE

BIG FOOT.

When you think it over, nothing is as good as mutton stew. But I am more partial, on a wonderful day when it is snowing hard, to having it boiled or well done à la bourguignon by the meticulous and jealous care of my cook, the Hispano-mauresque Slav slave, my albuminous servant and mistress, melting into the fragrant architecture of the kitchen. Apart from the pitch and the glue of her attentions, nothing can equal her allure and her chopped flesh on the dead calm of her regal movements. Her sprightly jokes, her warmth and her chill stuffed with hatred are nothing more, in the middle of a meal, than the goad of desire larded with gentleness. The cold of her nails turned against herself and the searing fire of her lips, frozen on the straw of the open dungeon, removes nothing of its character from the scar of the wound. The chemise lifted from beauty, her gaudy charm, anchored to her blouse, and the tidal force of her favours, shake off the golden powder of her glances into the nooks and the corners of the sink, stinking of laundry hung out to dry at the window of her looks, sharpened with the whetstone of her tangled hair. And if the Aeolian harp of her foul and common language and her laugh, trouble the polished surface of this portrait, it is due to her immoderate proportions and her disturbing propositions that she receives this avalanche of admiration. The spear from the bouquet of flowers, which she gathers in the air as she passes, shouts in her hands the royal acclamation of the victim. The galloping pace of his love crystallized into thought, the canvas born each morning in the fresh egg of her nakedness jumps the barrier and falls panting on the bed. I have such marks on my body; they are alive, they shout and sing and prevent me from catching the 8.45. The roses of her fingers smell of turpentine. When I listen at the ear of silence and see her eyes close, spreading the perfume of her caresses, I light the candles of sin with the match of her charms. The electric cooker can take the blame.

*

SCENE TWO

(Knocking at the door)

ROUND PIECE.
Somebody there?

BIG FOOT.
Come in!

ROUND PIECE.
It is very comfortable in your place, Big Foot, old man, and what a good smell of roast sucking pig!
Goodnight, and I'm going. But crossing the Bridge of

Sighs I saw a light in your place and I dropped in to give you your ticket for tonight's draw in the national lottery.

BIG FOOT.
Thank you. Here is the money. This is the sort of luck I had this morning, at biscuit time with figs, half fig, half grape, and so fresh. One more day and its black glory ...

ROUND PIECE.
It's cold!

BIG FOOT.
Would you like a glass of water? That will warm your guts. This business of house letting preoccupies and saddens me because of the landlord, the good fat old Jules, agrees about the price and the fees, the neighbour from across the way, that bitch, worries me. Her fat cat never stops prowling round my cage of mice and I can see the moment coming when the tropical fish that I feed to them alive, will be torn to shreds and devoured by that stupid brute. My frogs of the tube-game are in good health, but the aloe wine that I made has gone bad; and I cannot see this winter ending without greater shortages awaiting us.

ROUND PIECE.
The quickest way would be to put a small dead mouse on the end of a solid fish-hook and dragging the line gently on the end of a stick, lie down and wait until the fat cat is caught. Kill it, skin it, cover it completely with feathers, teach it to sing and mend watches. After that you could roast it and make yourself a vegetable broth.

BIG FOOT.

> He who laughs last, laughs best. The cat dead, and the person I love come to wish me a happy new year, the house will shine like a lantern and the feasting will burst all the strings of the violins and the guitars.

ROUND PIECE.

> Madness! Madness! Madness! Men are mad. The sash of the veil that hangs from the eyelashes of the shutters wipes pink clouds on the apple-coloured mirror of the sky, which awakens already at your window. I am off to the café at the corner to tear off with my claws the remains of the chocolate colour that still prowls in the blackness of its coffee. A very good morning to you, till tomorrow evening, see you soon!

(He goes out)

*

SCENE THREE

(BIG FOOT lies down on the ground in the middle of the stage and begins to snore. Enter from both sides of the stage THE ANXIETIES, THE COUSIN and THE TART)

THIN ANXIETY. (Looking at BIG FOOT)

> He is as beautiful as a star. He is a dream repainted in water colour on a pearl. His hair has the complicated arabesques of the halls in the palace of the Alhambra and his complexion has the silver

sound of the bell that rings the evening tango in my ears so full of love. His whole body is full of the light of a thousand shining electric lamps. His trousers are swollen with all the perfumes of Arabia. His hands are transparent mirrors made of peaches and pistachios. The oysters of his eyes enclose hanging gardens gaping at the words of his glances, and the garlic mayonnaise colour which encircles him sheds such a gentle light on his breast that the song of birds that is heard sticks to it like a squid to the mast of a fishing smack which, in the swell of my blood, navigates according to his image.

FAT ANXIETY.
I would like to have a go at him without his knowing.

THE TART. (With tears in her eyes)
I love him.

THE COUSIN.
I knew a gentleman in Chateauroux, an architect who wore spectacles and who wanted to keep me. A very nice and a very rich gentleman. He would never allow me to pay for my dinner and in the afternoon, between seven and eight, he would have an appetizer at the big café on the corner of the high street. It was he who taught me to carve a lemon sole. Afterwards, he went away for good, to live in an old historic castle. Well, myself, I find that lying like that on the floor and sleeping, they look exactly alike.

THE TART. (Throwing herself on top of him and weeping)
I love him, I love him.

(THE TART, THE COUSIN and THE TWO ANXIETIES each take big scissors from their pockets and begin to

cut locks of his hair, until they have stripped his head
like a Dutch cheese known as 'The Death's Head'.
Through the slats in the shutters of the window whips
of sunlight begin to beat the four women seated round
BIG FOOT)

THE TART.
Aye aye aye aye aye aye aye.

THE COUSIN.
Aye aye aye aye ...

THIN ANXIETY.
Aye aye aye aye aye ...

FAT ANXIETY.
A A A A A A A A A ...

(And that goes on for a good quarter of an hour)

BIG FOOT. (Dreaming)
The marrow bone carts along blocks of ice.

THE COUSIN.
Oh isn't he beautiful! Aye aye aye ... who aye ... oh!
who aye aye is aye aye aye aye ... bo bo.

FAT ANXIETY.
A aa bo a a bo bo.

THE TART.
Aye aye I love him. Aye aye love bo bo aye aye aye
love him aye aye bo bo bo bo.

(They are covered with blood and fall fainting to the
ground)

(THE CURTAINS, opening their folds in front of this disastrous scene, immobilise their vexation behind a spread of unfolded cloth.)

*

ACT FOUR

SCENE ONE

(Stamping of feet)

THE TART.
> I'm going to win! You see, I'm going to win!

THE COUSIN.
> Me too! Me too! Me too!

FAT ANXIETY.
> I'll be first! It will be me the first!

BIG FOOT.
> I shall hit the jackpot.

ROUND PIECE.
> I shall get it!

THE ONION.
> Every time, I shall be first, you see, I shall be the first!

SILENCE.
> You will see, you will see!

THIN ANXIETY.
> My little finger has told me!

(The lottery wheel turns)

THE COUSIN.
7. That's luck! I hit the jackpot!

ROUND PIECE.
24. Plus 00.10.42. But I hit the jackpot, too! That makes 249 thousand 00 89.

FAT ANXIETY.
9. It's my number all right that wins the jackpot.

THE TART.
60, plus 200, and thousand, and 007. I win it, the jackpot for me too! I have always been lucky.

BIG FOOT.
4,449, good god! Here we are, millionaire, at the top of the list.

SILENCE.
1,800. Goodbye, misery, milk, eggs and dairymaid! Here I am master of the jackpot.

ROUND PIECE.
4,254. Jackpot winner I am, congratulate myself.

THE COUSIN.
0009. I am the jackpot winner! I'm the jackpot winner! I am the jackpot winner!

THE ONION.
3,924. I win the jackpot! That's correct.

FAT ANXIETY.
11. That's the jackpot that I win!

THIN ANXIETY.
   17,215. I've got the jackpot everywhere!

THE CURTAINS. (Shaking themselves like madmen)
   1. 2. 3. 4. We win the jackpots! We win the jackpots!
   We win the jackpots!

   (A great silence lasts for some minutes, during which
   in the prompter's box, over a big fire in a big frying
   pan, potatoes are seen, heard and smelt frying in
   boiling oil; the fumes of the chips fill the room more
   and more until complete suffocation follows.)

*

ACT FIVE

ACT FIVE

SCENE ONE

BIG FOOT. (Half stretched out on a camp bed, writing)
'Fear of the uneven temper of love and tempers of the
leaping goat of madness. Covering laid over azure
released from the seaweed that covers the dress
starched with rich scraps of flesh brought to life by the
presence of puddles of pus from the woman who has
suddenly appeared reclining on my bed. Gargle of the
molten metal from her hair shouting with pain all her
joy of being possessed. Random game of crystals
imbedded in the melted butter of her dubious gestures.
The letter that follows step by step the word inscribed
on the lunar calendar hanging by its folds from the
brambles breaks open the egg filled with hatred and
the tongues of fire of her will set in the pallor of a lily
at the exact moment when the exasperated lemon
melts with delight. Double game of knuckle bones
painted with the same red as the border of her cloak,
the gum arabic which drips from the calm of her
attitude breaks the harmony of the deafening noise of
silence caught in a trap.

The reflection of her grimaces painted on the mirror
open to the winds perfumes the hardness of her blood
on the cold flight of the doves that receive it. The
blackness of ink envelops the rays of the sun's saliva
hitting on the anvil the lines of the drawing, bought at

the price of gold develop, in the needle-point of the desire to take her in his arms, his acquired strength and his illicit powers to win her. I run the risk of having her dead in my arms, ripe and mad.' Love letter, if you like. Quickly written and quickly torn up. Tomorrow or this evening or yesterday, I will have it posted by the devoted care of my friends. Cigarette 1, cigarette 2, cigarette 3, one, two, three, one plus two plus three equals six cigarettes; one smoked, another grilled and the third roasted on the spit before the fire. Hands hanging around the neck like a rope let down in haste from a tree that flies away whip relentlessly her classic figure of a half-baked Venus. Both feet together, the day lowers the weight of these years into the pit, full of shadow. The guts dragged by Pegasus after the fight draw her portrait, on the whiteness and hardness of the gleaming marble of her pain.

The noise of unfastened shutters hitting their drunken bells on the crumpled sheets of the stones tears from the night despairing cries of pleasure. The hammer blows of flowers and the sweet stink from her tresses season the stew of her bay leaves and cloves. Flying hands, hands detached from the laced sleeves of the bodice placed and folded with such care on the velvet of the chair, propped so roughly against the cheeks of the axe planted on the block, copy mournfully in a fine round hand the lesson which has been learnt. Stone hardened with anemones that devour the quicklime of the curtain that sleeps on the ladder leaning against the sulphur of the sky hung to the window frame. The most valid reasons, the imminence of peril, the dread and the desires which drive her do not prevent her at a time of morose joy like this settling down comfortably at home on the 'hope-green' sofa.

THE TART. (Enters, running)
Good morning! Good morning! I bring you an orgy. I
am all naked and I am dying of thirst. Will you please
make me a cup of tea at once and some honey on
toast. I am ravenous and so hot! Please allow me to
make myself at home. Give me a fur full of moths so
that I may cover myself. And to start with, kiss me on
the lips, and here, here, here and there and
everywhere. Isn't it clear that I must love you, to have
come like this in slippers, like a neighbour and all
naked to say good morning and make you believe that
you love me and want to have me close to you,
darling little sweetheart that I am to you and absolute
mistress of my thoughts for you, such a tender adorer
of my charms you would seem to be. Don't be so
embarrassed, give me another big kiss. And a thousand
more. Go on now, go and make me some tea. And
meanwhile I am going to cut the corn on my little toe
that annoys me.

(BIG FOOT takes her in his arms and they fall to the
ground)

THE TART. (Getting up after the embrace)
You're smart enough at giving and taking. I'm covered
with snow and shivering. Bring me a hot brick!

(She squats in front of the prompter's box, and facing
the audience, pisses and pisses scalding hot for a good
ten minutes)

THE TART.
Oof! That's better now!

(She farts, she farts again, she tidies her hair, sits
down on the floor and begins a clever demolition of
her toes.)

BIG FOOT. (Enters again, holding a big account book
     under his arm)
     Here is your tea. No water in the tap. No tea. No
     sugar. No cup nor saucer. No spoon. No glass. No
     bread and no jam. But here under my arm I have a
     fine surprise: **my novel**, and from this great sausage I
     am going to cut you some thick slices, that I shall stuff
     into your head, if you will allow me and are willing to
     listen to me very attentively, during a few of these
     long years of blackest night that we are spending
     together cheerfully, this morning until midday. Now
     here is page 380,000, which to me appears to be
     seriously of interest.

(He reads)

'The acrid stench spread around the concrete fact of
the narrative, established **a priori**, does not pledge the
person destined to this task to the slightest modesty. In
the presence of his wife and before a public notary,
we, the only responsible person established known
and honourably recognised as author, I pledge my
entire responsibility only in the specific case when
unbounded anxiety may become fanatical and
murderous for the limited view of the subject at table,
expatiating at full capacity, on the plumb-line of the
complex machine for establishing at any price the
exact data of this case already experimented by others,
contrary to the light cast by points of view on how to
support the weight of these interior precisions.' 'The
armoured ball-room was full of the sugar and the
brine of beauty and the best of the darlings of select
society seated facing reality full of the purple feathers
of children thrown to the winds like out of date and
worm-eaten tears.' 'On the regimental clock tower,
the clock advertised the most complete indifference to
the angles of the sundial held at its waist. The

titillations of crows that make the jagged wheel of the
machine for sewing and unsewing buttons, animates
the half dead landscape so little that grass grows over
their flight and at the shadows carried by their wings
fail to stick on the wall of the church but slip along the
cobble stones of the square, where they break to
pieces in a satisfactory realisation of the adventure
which is destined to occupy this provisional
pigeonhole.'

THE ONION and THE COUSIN. (Entering)
Oy ... We have brought you some shrimps! Oy ...
look here ... we have brought you some shrimps!

BIG FOOT.
That's delightful; here we are having a quiet fuck and
you come and annoy us with your filthy shrimps. How
do you expect us, Onion and you, Cousin, to care a
damn for your shrimps?

THE COUSIN.
What! rosy shrimps! Flowers! You call that 'our filthy
shrimps! We are kind, we think of you and you swear
at us. That isn't nice.

THE ONION.
That'll teach me next time to offer you shrimps.

BIG FOOT.
No, but sometimes ...

THE COUSIN.
You, Tart, this time I shall go straight and tell your
mother everything. This is fine and dandy! All naked
in front of a gentleman, an author, a poet ... and all
naked in your stockinged feet, it may be very
highbrow and very saucy, but that will not make you

a Venus, nor a muse, nor give you the manners expected of a respectable girl. What will your mother say when this evening at the laundry she is certain to hear about this shocking, shameless behaviour of a trollop dragged in the gutter of **Big Foot's Artistic Studio** by her lewd desires?

THE TART.
   Cousin, you're a curse ... and, by the way, have you any cotton-wool, or lend me your handkerchief? I shall go and tidy myself and then go out. I'm off. I'm going home. Really this man is a pig, a pervert, a libertine and a Jew.

(She goes into the bathroom)

BIG FOOT.
   Now that the Tart is gone, listen to me. That girl is mad and is trying to impress us with her affected tricks like a princess. I love her, of course, and she pleases me. But between that and making her my wife, my muse or my Venus, there is still a long and difficult path to reconnoitre. If her beauty excites me and I am mad about her stench, her table manners, her way of dressing and her affectations are a pain in the arse. Now, tell me frankly what you are thinking. I am listening. You, Cousin, what do you think?

THE COUSIN.
   I know her very well, your little friend. We were bosom friends at school for several years. And I can assure you that her conduct during lessons was held up to us as an example. If she was covered with spots, of course I knew all about that, that was not her fault, but because of a lack of various fats and the negligence of a girl, abandoned entirely by her instincts. Very dirty in her person, untidy hair, stinking of a thousand

nasty smells and sleepy. In her short black apron, her heavy slippers and her knitted jacket, all the men – old workmen, young men and gentry, we could see clearly the fires and the candles lighted before her devastating image that they carried away, the pure diamond of the fountain of youth burning in hands hidden in their trouser pockets.

THE ONION.
That child for me had the flavour of angelica.

THE COUSIN.
Now, there's no denying it! The Tart is a big girl and quite a pretty girl.

BIG FOOT.
Her body is a summer night overflowing with light and the perfume of jasmine and stars.

THE ONION.
You like her, Big Foot. Big Foot, that is your business. If you like her, that's fine, and yours the luck, good and rotten. Courage! I give you my blessing. And good luck and plenty of it! Are you coming, Cousin? We are off. Well! Big Foot, no grudge against me ... The shrimps, don't forget to put in, specially, a big piece of bacon rind, parsley and good glassful of donkey's milk.

THE COUSIN.
... 'Night, Big Foot!

(They go out)

BIG FOOT.
What a set of pitiful cunts.

(He lies on the bed and begins to write again)

'The soft blue of the bow which covers with its lace veil the roses of the naked body of a wild amaranth in a cornfield soaks up drop by drop, the load of little bells from lemon-yellow shoulders beating their wings. Already the Demoiselles d'Avignon have an income of thirty-three long years.'

THE TART. (Comes out of the bathroom dressed and wearing a hat of the latest style)
What, they have gone? Without saying a word. French leave. May I tell you all these people disgust me! As for me, I love only you. But we must be good, my great big everything. Now that I am really a virgin, I am off straight away to put up the luminous signs of my breasts within reach of everybody, and feather my love-nest in the all night city market.

BIG FOOT. (Stretched on his bed and feeling underneath for the pot which cannot be found)
I carry in my worn-out pocket the candy sugar umbrella with outspread angles of the black light of the sun.

ACT SIX

SCENE ONE

(The scene takes place in the main sewer bedroom kitchen and bathroom of the villa of THE ANXIETIES)

THIN ANXIETY.

The burn made by my unhealthy passions stokes the wound of the chilblains enamoured of the prism which has come to stay on the mauve angles of the rainbow and evaporates it in confetti. I am nothing but a congealed soul, stuck to the window-panes of the fire. I beat my portrait against by brow and cry the merchandise of my pain, at windows, closed to all mercy. My chemise, torn to shreds by fans starched with my tears, bites the seaweed of my arms with the nitric acid of its blows dragging my dress at my feet and my cries from door to door. The little bag of sweets that I bought yesterday for Big Foot for 40 centimes burns my hands. Festering fistula in my heart, love plays marbles between the feathers of his wings. The old sewing machine which turns the horses and the lions of the tangled merry-go-round of my desires chops up my sausage flesh and offers it alive to the ice cold hands of stillborn stars, tapping on the panes of my window their wolfish hunger and their oceanic thirst. The enormous pile of logs waits resigned to its fate. Let us make the soup.

(Reading from a cookery book)

A half quarter of Spanish melon, some palm oil, some lemon, some broadbeans, salt, vinegar, breadcrumbs; simmer gently; skim off as it rises, any soul likely to go to hell; cool off; print off a thousand copies on Japanese Imperial and let it congeal in time to give it to the squids.

(Shouting down the sewerhole of their bed)

Sister! Sister! Come here! Come and help me to lay the table and to fold this dirty linen stained with blood and excreta! Hurry up, sister, the soup is already cold and melts on the bottom of the looking glass on the wardrobe. All afternoon I have embroidered in this soup a thousand stories which it is going to whisper in secret in your ear, if you will kindly keep until the end of the bouquet's architecture some violets for the skeleton.

FAT ANXIETY. (All dishevelled and black with dirt, rising from the bed linen full of potato chips, holding an old frying pain in her hand)
I come from far away and am dazzled by the great patience that I had to sustain behind the hearse, jumping like the carp that the fat dyer and cleaner, who is so exact in his accounts, tried to place at my feet.

THIN ANXIETY.
The sun.

FAT ANXIETY.
Love.

THIN ANXIETY.
Aren't you beautiful!

FAT ANXIETY.

When I left this morning from the sewer of our house, immediately, just outside the gate, I took off my heavy pair of hob-nailed shoes from my wings and, plunging into the icy pond of my sorrows, I let myself drift in the waves far from shore. Lying on my back, I stretched myself out on the filth of that water and for a long time I held my mouth wide open to catch my tears. My closed eyes also received the crown of that long rain of flowers.

THIN ANXIETY.

Dinner is ready.

FAT ANXIETY.

Here is to mirth, love and the spring!

THIN ANXIETY.

Come along, carve the turkey and help yourself properly to the stuffing. The great bouquet of terrors and of frights already begins to wave us goodbye. And the mussel shells chatter their teeth, dying of fear under the frozen ears of boredom.

(She takes a piece of bread, which she dips into the sauce)

There is not enough salt and pepper in this slop. My aunt had a canary which sang old drinking songs all night.

FAT ANXIETY.

I shall help myself to some more sturgeon. The bitter erotic savour of these delicacies keeps my depraved taste for spiced and raw dishes panting eagerly.

THIN ANXIETY.
I found just now the white lace dress that I wore at the White Ball which was given me on that disastrous day, my birthday, all moth-eaten and covered with stains, on the top of the W.C. cupboard, writhing in burning pain under the dust of the ticktock of the grandfather clock. Without doubt our char must have worn it the other day to go and see her man.

FAT ANXIETY.
Look, the door comes running towards us. There is someone inside it who is coming in. The postman? No, it is the Tart.

(Speaking to THE TART)

Come in. Come and eat with us. You must be happy. Tell us the latest about Big Foot. The Onion came here this morning, pale and in despair, soaked in urine and wounded, pierced through the forehead with a pickaxe. He was weeping. We cared for him and consoled him as best we could. But he was in pieces. He was bleeding everywhere and screaming incoherent words like a lunatic.

THIN ANXIETY.
Do you know, the cat had her kittens last night.

FAT ANXIETY.
We drowned them in a hard stone, to be exact in a beautiful amethyst. It was fine this morning. A bit cold, but hot all the same.

THE TART.
You know, I have found love. He has all the skin worn off his knees and goes begging from door to door. He hasn't got a farthing, and is looking for a job as a

suburban bus conductor. It is sad, but go to his help
... he'll turn on you and sting you. Big Foot wanted to
have me and it is he who is caught in the trap. Look! I
have been out in the sun too long, I am covered with
blisters. Love. Love ... Here is half a crown, change it
for me into dollars and keep for yourselves the crumbs
of small change. Goodbye! For ever. Happy birthday,
my friends! Good evening! A very good day to you!
Happy new year and goodbye!

(She lifts up her skirts, shows her behind and
laughing, jumps with one bound through the window,
breaking all the panes)

FAT ANXIETY.
A pretty girl, intelligent, but peculiar. All that will
come to a bad end.

THIN ANXIETY.
Call everybody.

(She takes a trumpet and sounds the 'Fall In'. All the
characters of the play come running)

You, Onion, come forward. You are entitled to six
drawing room chairs. Here they are.

THE ONION.
Thank you madam!

FAT ANXIETY.
Big Foot, to you, if you can answer my questions, I
shall give the hanging lamp from the dining room. Tell
me, how much does four and four make?

BIG FOOT.
Too much and not a great deal.

THIN ANXIETY.
> Very good!

FAT ANXIETY.
> Very good!

THIN ANXIETY. (Uncorking a bottle and holding it under
the nose of ROUND PIECE)
> Round Piece, of what does this smell?

(ROUND PIECE laughs)

THIN ANXIETY.
> Very good! You've guessed. Here is this box full of
> quill pens. They are for you. And good luck.

FAT ANXIETY.
> Tart, show us your accounts.

THE TART.
> I have 600 litres of milk in my breasts of a sow. Some
> ham. Some streaky bacon. Some liver sausage. Some
> tripe. Some blood sausage. And my hair covered with
> chippolatas. I have mauve gums, sugar in my urine
> and white of egg all over my hands, gnarled with gout.
> Bony cavities. Bile. Cankers. Fistulas. The King's evil.
> And lips twisted with honey and marshmallows.
> Clothed with decency, clean, I wear with elegance the
> ridiculous dresses that are given me. I am a mother
> and perfect whore and I can dance the rumba.

THIN ANXIETY.
> You shall have a can of petrol and a fishing rod. But
> first, you must dance with us all. Start with Big Foot.

(Music plays, and they all dance, changing partners all
the time)

BIG FOOT.
Let us wrap the worn-out sheets in the face-powder of angels and turn the mattresses inside out in the brambles. Light all the lanterns. Throw flights of doves with all our strength against the bullets and lock securely the houses demolished by bombs.

(ALL THE CHARACTERS come to a stop on either side of the stage. By the window at the end of the room bursting it open suddenly, enters a golden ball the size of a man which lights up the whole room and blinds the characters, who take handkerchiefs from their pockets and blindfold themselves and, stretching up their right arms, point at each other, shouting all together and many times)

ALL.
You! You! You!

(On the golden ball appear the letters of the word: 'Nobody'.)